EXTRAORDINARY SPRING

A Wartime Childhood in West Sussex

EXTRAORDINARY SPRING

A Wartime Childhood in West Sussex

Roy Gardner

The Book Guild Ltd
Sussex, England

The Book Guild
25 High Street,
Lewes, Sussex

First published 1997

© Roy Gardner, 1997

Set in Times
Typsetting by RGA Design. Hove, East Sussex

Printed in Great Britain by
Bookcraft (Bath) Ltd, Avon

A catalogue record for this book is
available from the British Library

ISBN 1 85776 166 9

To my grandchildren, Alexandra, Lydia, Richard and Rebecca I dedicate these words and hope that as you grow in stature and character and become citizens of the 21st century, you may enjoy recalling the story of a childhood far removed from your own and possibly benefit from reading an *Extraordinary Spring*.

Acknowledgements

May I express my sincere thanks to all who made the publication of this book possible.

Dame Vera Lynn, DBE for kindly writing the foreword.

Mrs Pat Smith, for deciphering my dreadful longhand and typing a legible manuscript.

John Hammond and Mick Canning of the *Worthing Herald*, for the photograph of evacuees and for tracing additional material.

Mrs P. Knight and Walter Gardiner Photography, for photographs of Worthing, circa 1940/41.

The Staff at Worthing Reference Library.

Chris Tod, Steyning Museum Trust, for the photograph of Elsie and Doris Waters.

Nicholas Burden for Victory Certificate.

The management and staff of The Book Guild Ltd, Lewes.

My mother, for her memories and for filling in the missing pages.

My wife, for her patience, tolerance and help with proof reading.

Finally, my three children for their persistent demands to tell them yet another wartime story.

Preface

The ages of man's life have been likened to the four seasons. As I approach the winter of my life it would seem appropriate to record for the posterity of my grandchildren and perhaps other interested parties, an account of an extraordinary childhood. A childhood totally remote and so often lacking the most fundamental things which children take for granted today.

I have attempted to recall events, exactly as they occurred, and trust that this narrative will afford you, dear reader amusement, pathos and possibly disbelief.

Foreword

DAME VERA LYNN D.B.E., LL.D., M.MUS.

I found this book very amusing and interesting and it brought back many memories to me, as I am sure it will to many who lived during that time.

It will also give the younger generation a very good idea what life was like living in the country during the War, with all its problems. These country days have long gone, I am sorry to say, but fortunately the memories remain.

Vera Lynn

Chapter One

My birthplace was devoid of the usual aseptic atmosphere associated with maternity hospitals and consisted of the bedroom immediately above the off-licence shop, of which my father was the manager.

I weighed in at slightly over 9lbs on the evening of the 7th December 1935. Nothing extraordinary in that, you might think, but as my mother finally ended a most difficult confinement, and I gave forth my first hearty cries, customers plonked their shillings and half-crowns down upon the wooden counter of the shop below and demanded replacement bottles of stout or ale from my anxious father.

My earliest recollection is lying in my cot listening to the harsh ting ting from the bell echoing through the open window, as the shop door opened and closed, announcing a new customer's arrival.

As I learnt to walk and understand the spoken word, I would sit on a small stool, slightly to the right of the counter, and watch my parents as they dealt and talked with the customers. Extraordinary words like "Hitler," "Mussolini," "Munich" and "Chamberlain," came drifting down to my place of observation, but were meaningless to my young ears. As I sat listening to, but not comprehending, this adult conversation, one particular word was repeatedly overheard -"WAR!" At four years of age this word meant nothing to me, but within a very short time I was to learn first hand the meaning of war, together with the ramifications which would follow.

The wail of the air raid siren would herald the approaching German bombers, as they flew overhead towards their target, usually London. The rattle of machine guns being fired overhead became commonplace, as did the staccato sound of the ack-ack gun firing only yards from our house.

Sleepless nights became the norm. When the siren sounded I would be hurriedly wrapped in a blanket by mother and taken with my sister to the community shelters built in the recreation ground near our home. I can recall the obnoxious smell of those damp underground shelters; water dripped everywhere and in winter the cold was penetrating. Even today, I loathe the odour of burning paraffin, which emitted from the hurricane lamps suspended from the ceiling or walls and provided the only source of light.

Blackout was compulsory from the early days of the war, requiring all windows and doors to be covered with a dark material, to prevent any light from showing through into the pitch black streets. Ours were made by my father from heavy gauge black cardboard, fastened to a light wooden frame and fixed to the window recess by means of small hooks and catches, every evening for nearly five years.

When the curtains were drawn across the blackout, not a chink of light showed through. Similarly, fresh air was excluded, making our small living room rather warm and stuffy in the depths of winter, especially with a coal fire burning.

If we ventured out after dark, we would carry a very small hand torch, its beam partly obscured by a black screen covering half of the glass. Vehicles were also fitted with screens covering their headlights, allowing only a tiny beam of light to shine through a small aperture. Lamp posts and telegraph poles were painted with white stripes around their bases, but this didn't prevent people walking into them in the darkness.

The ack-ack (anti-aircraft guns) were positioned along the south coast, including several near our home. We often used to visit these gun emplacements and sometimes the soldiers allowed us to sit on the seat and pretend to shoot down imaginary aircraft, as we swivelled the gun barrel around, our eye fixed to the gunsight aimed at a regrettably empty sky.

Huge searchlights, their beams probing and swaying into the darkened sky, would seek out enemy intruders who dared to violate our homes and country. Then all hell would appear to break loose, as every gun within the vicinity would open fire at the bomber, which twisted and turned to escape this blinding glare, like a moth trapped by a flame.

Mr Middleton, the radio gardener, encouraged us to "Dig for Victory" and grow our own food. My parents took this matter very seriously, even to the extent of dressing me up to look like the man himself, complete with pipe and trilby hat. To their astonishment and mine this enabled me to take first prize in a local fancy dress competition.

Aluminium from old pots and pans was collected en masse by local school children. We were assured that this, along with iron railings from parks and houses, would help build fighters and bombers.

My sister, Betty, and I made our own contribution by collecting money from customers as they left the shop for "Buy a Spitfire Fund". Rattling our tin under their noses and with a pleading look in our young eyes, never failed to raise 3d(1½p) or 6d(2½p) for our very worthy cause. At the end of three weeks we had amassed the enormous sum of £4.12s.9½d, which we felt must be a poke in the eye for Adolf Hitler.

The evacuees arrived one summer's afternoon in 1940 and I stood in the shop doorway, clutching my mother's skirt, watching the coach which had brought them from London, discharge its forlorn and tired young passengers, many only five or six years of age, onto the forecourt outside our home.

"Poor little beggars," said one of the WVS. (Women's Voluntary Service) women, who was supervising the children to their allotted billets.

"They look very pale and peaky don't they," said another, pointing at a boy about ten years of age, with a tubercular pallor.

The children milled around, clasping their gas mask cases and parcels of belongings, bewilderment and confusion etched on their young faces, as these strange ladies in green and maroon uniforms sorted them like livestock and handed them to complete strangers with a promise of 10/- (50p) per week for their upkeep.

One little girl with fair hair and pigtails, of about my age, perhaps slightly younger, was sobbing uncontrollably, whilst clutching tightly the hand of a boy about two years older, who I assumed was her brother. He pulled her hand away from his, reached inside a grubby carrier bag and pulled out a rather squashed looking bun, which he offered to her. She stopped crying for a few minutes, took the bun and then threw both arms around the little fellow's waist, and commenced sobbing into his shoulder as if her heart would break.

My mother left me standing in the shop doorway and went to comfort both children, who by now were both crying, confused and dismayed by their strange surroundings. As my mother gently soothed these two troubled children, I watched solemnly as one by one they were led away by their allotted families.

Mrs Smith, a friend of my mother's, was clearly upset by the distress caused to these children and, with tears in her eyes and her voice trembling with emotion, said, "What have these poor little mites done to deserve this? It will leave a scar on their young minds for the rest of their lives."

My mother said nothing, merely glancing back to see if I was still standing in the doorway. No doubt, my sister and I had our evacuee labels and name tabs already written, ready in case of us having to be sent away at short notice should the Nazi invaders come.

An unexplained mystery remains to this very day. Did the Germans attempt an invasion on the South Coast in 1940/41 or some form of commando operation, which went badly wrong? Many elderly people living today, including my 87-year-old mother, are convinced that a seaborne assault of some description did take place,

Author as Mr Middleton 1940

The evacuees' arrival
(Note gas mask cases and labels)

South Lancing Primary School, 1940
(Note anti-bomb blast tape at windows and
teacher's gas mask case in foreground)

and is surely worth recounting, in the belief that some day records may prove her correct.

The ARP headquarters were buzzing with rumours and denials at this time, the local police officer informing them that the blaze seen all along the seafront from our home was the result of the sea being set alight with petrol to deter and destroy the invaders. My late father often recalled that the light from seaward at 2 a.m. was strong enough to read a newspaper by.

Then rumours of badly burnt bodies being washed ashore filtered in. All of this was strongly denied by the authorities at the time, but still remains an unsolved mystery.

Incidentally, in the summer of 1994, an identity tag from a high ranking German officer was found on the beach at Hove. Coincidence? I wonder!

Blacked out streets and houses were accepted as normal, as were shortages of food, clothes and toys, the latter virtually disappeared as the war dragged on. Like children of any generation, we learned to adapt and, dare I say, war become a game second to none, unless someone known to us was killed or missing in action.

Hitler and Fatty Goering were just clowns whom we loved to impersonate, strutting about with our goose steps and "Heil Hitlers", and the ambition of most boys was to be a Spitfire pilot when they grew up.

On our way to school we would collect pieces of shrapnel lying in the road, which came from the ack-ack guns that fired at German bombers as they flew overhead.

All the windows in the school at South Lancing had anti-bomb blast tape criss-crossed over the glass and, should the air raid siren sound during lessons, we were quickly ushered into Anderson shelters dug out in the school grounds, later replaced by surface shelters built of reinforced concrete.

Collecting and swapping war souvenirs grew apace and we vied with one another to show the latest acquisitions. Live rounds of ammunition would be hidden in school desks to be passed around for perusal during playtime, until a horrified teacher confiscated them.

One day in early May1942 my mother and her friend Dorrie who, incidentally, was my best friend Michael's mother decided to take us in search of cowslips up on the nearby South Downs.

Neither Mike nor I were keen on picking flowers, and so we kicked a ball around aimlessly as our mums gossiped away, contemplating the latest ration cuts, or how to make Michael's shoes last that little bit longer, whilst chastising us for hastening their premature wear.

Suddenly, something glistening in the far corner of a ploughed field caught my eye and, with Michael running breathlessly behind me, we made haste to investigate this strange phenomenon.

Oh joy! Oh bliss! It couldn't be - but it really was. A large section of Jerry (German) aircraft, complete with Prussian cross, confronted our young, eager eyes and with shouts of,"Look what we've found mum!" echoing,we commenced to drag our booty home. With all thoughts of cowslips dashed from our minds, our sole aim was to bring our treasure back to our homes, all of two miles away!

After contemplating our excited faces, the two mothers decided to help. Dorrie removed the belt of her dress, which we quickly fastened through one of the many bullet holes, and the dragging began.

Pulling this large chunk of aluminium behind us proved rather more difficult than anticipated, not least because it often snagged in a furrow or rabbit hole. Eventually we came to the roadway and, as this was totally deserted of traffic, continued our towing operation along it.

The sound of metal grating over tarmac is extremely difficult to comprehend, and is best left to the imagination of the reader. As we passed by, doors were thrown open and people hurried to their gates first glaring, then laughing at us as the cause of the awful din was discovered.

Finally, we reached the gates at the side of the shop, and with one final heave our largest trophy to date, was ready to display to the local gang of street urchins, of which we were now top dogs.

"Swap you my Mills bomb for it!" exclaimed one boy.

"You can have my two incendiaries and some *Beanos* if you like!" said another lad, gazing longingly at the hunk of distorted metal.

For several days we were the envy of the neighbourhood. Then further pieces of this Heinkel bomber, which had been destroyed by one of our night fighters, were found scattered over a wide area. A large section of propeller was found on a bungalow roof, whilst the most gruesome find was a boot containing a severed foot, which a horrified lady discovered in her back garden.

To us children it was still a marvellous game, and the fact that the remains of the crew from the bomber had been buried in the cemetery at Sompting, meant little to our young minds, conditioned with but one aim: to beat the Nazis and win the war.

The authorities warned children against picking up strange objects found lying in the street or fields. Posters were pinned up in our school and elsewhere, depicting butterfly bombs and other such lethal devices, which were dropped by the Germans and which exploded when handled by personnel or curious children. However these warnings were usually totally ignored by us, sometimes with dangerous consequences.

My mother was busy tending the shop early one evening, when the door opened admitting the local newspaper boy, who had just completed his round. He reached inside the bag slung over his shoulder and calmly produced three incendiary bombs which he placed on the counter.

"Would you give these to Mr Gardner please Mrs!" exclaimed

this twelve year old to my rather startled mother. "I found them this morning," he continued, wiping his nose on the sleeve of his jacket. "Mr Gardner will know what to do wiv 'em!" he said and then started to leave.

"They've gone off of course?" asked my mother, staring at these three ominous metal objects complete with black metal fins.

"Course they 'ave'nt," answered the boy. "That's why I've brought them in for Mr Gardner to deal wiv," he retorted before closing the door behind him.

My father was deferred from military service owing to a damaged knee injury sustained during his youth. In view of this, he decided to volunteer for the ARP (Air Raid Precautions) or Wardens as they were known.

The large kitchen of our home doubled as the local headquarters of the ARP and with Wardens constantly coming and going during the nightly air raids, my mother was kept busy brewing up mugs of cocoa to sustain these volunteers as they went about their duties.

One of my father's jobs was to distribute hundreds of gas masks to the families in our area, and I was selected to model the children's respirators, including the so-called Mickey Mouse model made from blue and red rubber, as opposed to the black for the adults.

Small toddlers would scream and be terrified as these monstrosities were forced over their heads, so I was taken along to show them that there was nothing to fear - I blew raspberries or rude farting sounds through the nose piece, at these bemused youngsters.

The respirators, to give them their correct title, were even supplied for babies, and the infants would also howl and kick as they were placed inside the contraptions, leaving just their legs exposed when the tapes were tied together. It would seem ironic that the manufacturer of these horrors which, thank God, were never used, was a firm by the name of *Frankenstein*.

Boss Hart, the local rag-and-bone man, was constantly being

tormented and teased by the children, who loved nothing better than to run after his horse and cart, piled high with dirty old clothes and rubbish, and imitate his cry: "Rag, bone". "Rag, bone. Any rabbit skins?"

We would pull faces and stick out our tongues at this figure of fun, who ignored our taunts and cruelty.

On consulting our list of recipients for the gas masks, my father was somewhat dismayed to see that the Hart family were next on his rounds and, with some apprehension, he rang the doorbell of the small two-up-two-down terraced house, which was the Hart's abode.

The bolts of the door were drawn back and the door opened to reveal the slight figure of Mrs Hart. I involuntarily pinched my nose together with my finger and thumb, expecting an overwhelming smell to hit me. My eyes opened wide in astonishment as the door opened fully revealing a very neat and tidy hallway, with highly polished linoleum and a bright rug on the floor.

"Please come in," she said. "I will call the children in from the garden. Would you and your little boy like to wait in the front room."

My father and I were dumbfounded by the clean and well-furnished room which she escorted us into. As her children were led into the room one by one to be fitted with gas masks, I averted my gaze from their faces, especially the youngest, Ken, who was in my class at school and whom we had tormented unmercifully because of his parentage.

The entire family of five children were all spotlessly clean and, although their attire showed signs of wear, they were all extremely well-behaved and made no fuss when their respirators were slipped on.

Our surprise must have shown on dad's face and mine, for just as we were leaving, Mrs Hart said to my father, and obviously for my ears as well, that it was a pity that many children refused to play with her family and declined to make friends with them because of her husband's reputation.

"He wasn't always a rag-and-bone man," she went on, "and only started doing this after being shell-shocked in the First World War."

We said our goodbyes, feeling very humbled, and I knew that young Ken must be included in our gang at school forthwith.

Chapter Two

As the war dragged on, shortages of practically every commodity existed, and it was not uncommon during the winter months for the children to sit shivering in the classroom, without heating owing to either lack of coal, or most likely spare parts for the boiler.

Clothes became harder to obtain with each passing year. Make do and mend was the order of the day, or sometimes my sister and I would be taken to the WVS clothing exchange in Richmond Road, Worthing, known locally as the "Swap Shop". Here, our well-worn garments could be swapped for equally well-worn ones, but at least they made a change. Shoes became another problem but our salvation in this instance were Blakeys - metal studs of various shapes and sizes, which could be fastened to the soles and heels, adding extra life to shoes or boots until the uppers gave way in despair.

These studs provided an unexpected game for the children, for by running fast on a concrete surface then sliding with feet apart, sparks would issue forth beneath our feet, even more so when frost covered the ground on a winter's morning; great fun until you slipped and grazed your knees!

Coupons for this, points for that. The only thing we kids had aplenty on a daily basis was milk and cod liver oil, courtesy of the Ministry of Food and Health - yuk!

Concentrated orange juice was another delicacy supplied free of charge to the children by the Ministry of Food. This came in bottles of a similar shape and size to those for cod liver oil and I suspect that it was craftily mixed with the latter, judging by the thick oily substance which passed as orange juice when mixed with water and which we were encouraged to drink to keep us fit and healthy.

Fresh oranges were very rare and should a supply appear in the grocers, word soon got around and a long queue would form outside the shop. Mothers, children, and infants, clutched their blue and green ration books, which would be their passport to these citrus pleasures.

"Bananas", now there was a wonderful word in the 1940s. As with ice cream, these simple delights possessed a magical quality which children could only dream of - they appeared only when the war was over.

By mid 1941 the entire family were tired and weary, with nightly visits to the community shelter in the recreation ground and, as the majority of the bombers were making London and the larger cities their main targets, dad decided to construct a shelter for us in the narrow hallway of our home.

Using heavy timber for struts to reinforce the ceiling and walls and making bunks for us to sleep in, we were able to spend undisturbed nights sleeping in this fashion for many months, and ignored the wailing siren, which became commonplace.

As the winter of 1941 approached, there was considerable activity in the recreation ground. Convoys of army lorries arrived and huge camouflaged tents were erected, which were quickly occupied by hundreds of troops, all displaying "Canada" on their shoulder flashes.

The weather was atrocious as the weeks went by and my mother was appalled at the awful conditions in which these men were living. There was very little she could do for these "poor boys" as she called them, but felt that she had to do something. Our small cooker was continually brewing tea or cocoa, which somehow never seemed to run out, and dad and I, together with Bobby our dog, would make evening sorties across to the camp, laden with large enamel jugs of steaming brew.

The soldiers always seemed grateful for our small contribution and we would be invited to stay and share it with them. They always made a great fuss over Bobby, our cross-terrier, and appeared to make him their mascot. Bobby in turn, adored all this extra attention and would often run unaccompanied across to the recreation ground when the shop door was left open.

As the winter gave way to spring, the soldiers training intensified and we were often refused entry to the camp.

One evening in August 1942 their commanding officer appeared in the shop to personally thank mum and dad for their kindness during the winter months, and explained that they would be leaving very shortly.

Just a few days later there was much activity with the tents being taken down and lorries constantly rumbling away. On the evening of their departure, dad opened the shop door to wave goodbye to our Canadian friends, all now wearing full battle dress and carrying a variety of weapons. Before he could stop him, Bobby ran out of the doorway and bolted along the road after the receding army lorries. Dad's last glimpse of our dog, was of him leaping into the back of a lorry with the troops inside grabbing for his collar.

The following morning I came into the kitchen, expecting to see Bobby in his usual place, dozing beside the warm gas stove.

"Where's Bobby Mum?" I asked, noticing his bowl of biscuits and water untouched.

"Bobby's gone," answered my mother, turning her head away and avoiding my gaze.

"Gone where?" I questioned again, imploringly, pulling at her skirt with my hand and sensing something was wrong.

Just then my father entered the room and, taking me aside said very gently. "I'm afraid Bobby decided he wanted to go with his soldier friends last night. I'm sure they will take good care of him."

"But he's my dog, dad," I whined, starting to sob, the tears rolling down my cheeks.

"I know son, I know," said dad, holding both of my hands and trying to comfort me. "I expect they will bring him back very soon, so don't you worry now."

With this slight possibility as a small consolation, I stopped crying and then said innocently, "Where have the soldiers gone now dad?"

"I wish I knew son, but perhaps we shall soon find out," he answered, still trying to reassure me.

Just a few days later we learnt from the radio where Bobby and our Canadian friends had gone. Dieppe, hailed at that time as a successful combined operation, albeit a costly and bloody one, with half of the force killed or taken prisoner.

With the Yanks' and Canadians' arrival, a new delicacy appeared on our plates - spam and dried egg. Just a few spoons of dried egg made the world's largest omelette!

"Got any gum chum?" was our new catch phrase to these soldiers from over there and we pestered them for their *Sweet Caporal* cigarette packets, which had aircraft recognition pictures printed on them.

Occasionally we were reminded of what war was really about. Lancing Railway Carriage Works (now Churchill Industrial Estate) received a direct hit just as we were leaving school. Terrified youngsters threw themselves down in the wet playground as a Nazi bomber roared overhead.

The Carriage Works was in those days the main employer in the area, apart from nurseries or market gardens, and was often singled out for attention from the Luftwaffe, possibly because of hush hush work being carried out within.

The attack by the German bomber was at that time dubbed the miracle of Lancing. Had the bombs fallen fifteen minutes earlier, the factory area destroyed would have been full of workers, and would

Lancing Railway Carriage Works
(Now Churchill Industrial Estate)

Bomb Damage South Street, Lancing
(Now Bell Memorial Home)

The milk was delivered by horse and cart
(Highfield and Oaklands Dairies)

Our van in central Worthing
(Note air raid shelter)

have resulted in many casualties.

The works' hooter had sounded at twelve noon to announce lunch and the exodus to the canteen was in full swing as the bombs fell, destroying one of the main workshops. One lone worker taking refuge beneath a bench, was dug out from under the rubble suffering little more than severe shock. At the time, many Lancing mothers ran terrified towards our school, believing we had been hit, only to find that it was their husbands and fathers who had been the targets. Their anxiety and anguish before the truth was known, can be imagined.

On another occasion, as I walked home with my mother, a drone of aircraft engines was heard. As the sound grew louder, I looked up and perceived a twin-engined aircraft emerging from the clouds.

"That's a Jerry up there Mum!" I exclaimed.

"Don't be silly dear. It must be one of ours, the siren hasn't gone!" she answered.

No sooner had she uttered these words than two black objects descended, as if in slow motion, from beneath the aircraft. As we stood rooted to the spot, the two bombs struck home, causing the ground upon which we stood to vibrate with the impact.

A vast amount of earth, flame and smoke billowed skywards, followed by the detonation seconds later. My mother stood transfixed with shock, and looked down at me vaguely, not comprehending the enormity of these explosions or my triumphant cry:

"Told you that was a bloomin' Jerry, Mum!" said I, as the belated siren began its mournful wail.

Conversations in the shop adopted a new tone with the arrival of Canadian and American troops in 1942/43 but they would often suddenly cease when I came within earshot.

"She's all of six months gone! The brazen hussy," caught my young ears, as I reached the doorway. For the life of me I couldn't make out why the very pretty young Landgirl, to whom they were referring, was supposed to be away somewhere, when I had seen her ride by only that very morning on her bicycle. She did have long red hair, however, so perhaps that explained the brazen bit. Mind you, I had noticed that she'd put on rather a lot of weight despite the rationing, but I expect she nibbled a bit when she was working in the fields.

AUTC (anything under the counter) was an oft used expression when shopping, and the off-licence was no exception. Whisky and gin were like gold dust and it was not for me to question where the box of tomatoes or newly shot wild rabbit came from. Dad was often overheard saying that he would see what he could do for these very benevolent customers, as they pleaded with abject humility.

"Just half a bottle of White Horse would be so much appreciated, Mr Gardner. By the way, does your family like mushrooms?"

Some of our deliveries were made by Sid on our Raleigh trade bicycle. It was his ambition to join the Royal Navy and, upon reaching seventeen years of age, he volunteered his services. Nothing was heard from him for some time, until his excited mother came into the shop proudly exclaiming that Sid's ship, HMS *Duke of York* had sunk the German cruiser *Sharnhorst.*

Other parents known to us were less fortunate. Their eighteen - year - old son, who delivered for the local butcher, was called up by the RAF, to serve as a rear gunner in Lancaster bombers.

"We're going to give those bastards what for! You'll see!," he told my mother one morning, as she swept the shop doorstep. I'm on my way back to base now, see you on my next leave," he called out, swinging his kitbag over his shoulder.

Just a few days later we learned from his distraught parents that he was missing in a raid over Germany, and tragically he never returned.

Our replacement thirteen-year-old delivery boy, whose name

escapes me, joined my sister, mother and I, as we took cover in the Morrison shelter, during a raid one damp afternoon in 1943.

As he crawled on all fours into the shelter, shivering with fear and cold, shaking rainwater and slivers of glass over us, my mother asked anxiously, "Whatever happened to you?"

"A bomb dropped when I was on my rounds!" he explained, brushing more glass from his mac.

"Why on earth didn't you take cover dear," said my mother gently, whilst trying to calm him down.

"I did just as Mr Gardner taught me and threw myself underneath the wall of Mrs Phillips' shop, when the raid started," he said, beginning to sob.

"Well, you should have been safe enough there!" said my mother.

"That's what I thought!" said the boy, brushing more rainwater and glass over us, recovering his composure. "But then there was a big bang and the blinkin' window fell out!"

The milkman and baker still delivered by horse-drawn cart, and as fuel became scarce, various forms of transport appeared, including a steam driven lorry which arrived one morning to deliver the shop's meagre supplies.

The hourly bus service which stopped immediately outside our home, resorted to gas. This was contained in a weird contraption on two wheels which was towed behind the Southdown vehicle. It had the appearance of a boiler, with various rubber pipes leading from it which were connected to the engine.

The droppings from the horses were eagerly awaited by the neighbourhood to enrich their plots of vegetables, and it was often a race to see who could collect these offerings first, with their spade and galvanized bucket.

One day my mother was busy preparing blackcurrant and apple jelly, and I watched intrigued as she squeezed the fruit through butter muslin into the jars. The residue she would drop into a container to

17

be thrown later onto the compost heap.

When she left the room I couldn't resist picking up handfuls of this gunge and rolling it into sizeable balls. Happily engrossed in my new found delight, I was unaware of my father entering the room.

"What on earth are those things you're making?" he laughed. "Hors d'Oeuvres?"

What I thought he said was "Horses- Doovers," and this gave me an idea! When it got dark I hurried outside and with my sister's help tipped a pile of our horses- doovers into the roadway.

The following morning we awoke early and sat patiently looking out of the front bedroom window to await events. We didn't have to wait very long. An elderly lady soon appeared with her bucket and shovel, bent down and then stopped with shovel poised, staring at the strange coloured mixture which met her eyes.

She called out to the milkman as he appeared around the corner, and he in turn went to examine the deposits left on the tarmac. Returning to his horse he lifted its tail, examined its rear carefully, then, scratching his head in bewilderment, proceeded to look at the contents of the horse's feed bag hanging on the cart.

By this time my sister and I were laughing so much that tears were running down our cheeks. Just then Mum appeared in the doorway.

"Have you two seen that bucket of waste I left for your father's allotment?" she demanded.

Chapter Three

Our parents performed wonders to provide my sister and me with happy Christmases during those dark years. Some two or three weeks prior to the festivities, my sister and I would make Christmas decorations from strips of coloured paper, and crackers, from discarded toilet rolls which we glued together with paste made from flour and water.

Beans from my father's allotment were salted down in jars, whilst plums and other soft fruits were preserved in large kilner jars. Dried apple rings were kept strung from the roof of the garden shed and would be used for the Christmas pudding along with the other ingredients. Dried fruit such as sultanas and raisins, were again in short supply so prunes were often used as an alternative.

On one occasion our local grocer advised my mother that he had received a small quota of mincemeat. In fairness, he had arranged for each customer to draw tickets from an empty biscuit tin.

Mum let me try my luck when it was her turn for the draw, and I rustled the tickets around carefully before withdrawing my hand. With bated breath, I slowly unfolded this important scrap of paper, and lo and behold the letter "M" for mincemeat confronted my eyes.

Never had mince pies tasted so good, as we sat munching them on Christmas Day 1942.

Wooden toys were made by my father for us, and my uncle also sent me a superb collection of small model aircraft, which he had carved with a pocket knife during long hours of sentry duty whilst serving with the army. These were kept well hidden from small prying eyes and would cause great delight on Christmas morning.

I well remember waking the entire household in the small hours, with the discovery of a Tommy Gun which dad had made. By turning a small handle connected to a grooved cotton reel, a realistic rat-a-tat-tat issued forth from my lifelike weapon.

Our delicious roast chicken dinner had, just a few days earlier, been strutting around in the run kept in the back garden, proudly keeping strangers away from his small brood of hens, which provided eggs for breakfast.

On the home front we listened nightly to our radio. Churchill's speeches were never interrupted by me or my sister, and Lord Haw Haw (William Joyce) made us laugh with his "Germany calling, Germany calling".

ITMA - It's That Man Again! with Tommy Handley was not to be missed, together with the following characters:

Colonel Chinstrap - "I don't mind if I do sir!"

Mrs Mopp (charlady) - "Can I do you now sir?"

Funf - "This is Funf speaking!" (we loved him) conjuring up pictures of Adolf again in our young minds.

TTFN - "Ta Ta For Now" was the catch phrase from this programme we all used when saying cheerio.

Other favourite Radio or Wireless personalities included Robb Wilton - "The day war broke out my Mrs said to me" ..... and Elsie and Doris Waters (Gert and Daisy).

Elsie and Doris Waters, who incidentally lived at Steyning, made numerous local appearances for charities and fetes, often giving impromptu performances for their legion of fans, nattering and gossiping about rationing, food shortages and not least, hubby Bert, serving with the Army somewhere overseas.

Vera Lynn
The Forces' sweetheart

Elsie and Doris Waters
Gert and Daisy

In real life Elsie and Doris were sisters of Jack Warner, later to find fame in the 50s and 60s, firstly in the film *The Blue Lamp*, then as TV's *Dixon of Dock Green*.

During the war, Jack kept us in stitches reciting his monologues about his "bruvver Sid," who had numerous dubious occupations, including my favourite, "a bunger up of rat 'oles".

Vera Lynn, the forces sweetheart, sang all our favourite tunes, and the song which appealed to most schoolboys was a tribute to our RAF heroes called "Coming in on a Wing and a Prayer".

Children's Hour was another nightly favourite on the radio, and Uncle Mac (Derek McCulloch) would always end the programme with his poignant phrase, "good night children everywhere" as if to remind the thousands of evacuees that they were not forgotten, as they struggled to come to terms with their foster families and alien surroundings, miles from home.

Our old wind-up gramophone provided hours of fun, although changing the needles after each record became an unwelcome chore. Many of these very fragile 78s had a patriotic theme, appealing to children of all ages. Much to our amusement, the words of "Run Rabbit, Run", sung by Flanagan and Allen, became "Run Adolf, run Adolf, run, run, run".

But what on earth dirty washing hanging on the Siegfried line had got to do with the war, was beyond my comprehension. Dad tried to explain that the Germans had marched around this line somewhere on the French/Belgium border, but I still failed to understand why this all-weather clothes line was supposed to hold up the German advance. Even my *Knockout* comic depicted this impregnable line on one occasion and, as if echoing my own thoughts, our Ernie's dad, Mr. Entwhistle, exclaimed from these absorbing pages, "Daft I calls it!"

Shoreham Airport was often under attack, especially in the early years of the war, and this was not entirely surprising.

Driving over the old wooden toll bridge which crossed the Adur north of the aerodrome one morning, dad and I were amazed to see what appeared to be large numbers of Spitfires and Hurricanes assembled on the outskirts of the airfield.

As we drew closer, there was something strange and unreal about this sudden increase in fighters. Slowing down for a better view, we realised straight away what was amiss with these aircraft, which swayed and shook in the rather strong breeze. Each and every one of them were dummies, made from plywood and canvas.

There was a sudden banging on the side of the van and a military policeman showed his face at the window.

"Move along please. This is a restricted area!" he said sternly, and so without further ado we drove hurriedly away.

Mike and I would often cycle along to do our plane spotting from the grassy banks adjoining the Sussex Pad Public House, close to the airfield. We became quite expert at identifying the different aircraft, and by 1943 knew most of them by heart. Our favourite without any doubt was the superb Spitfire, and we were delighted when a Free French Squadron was based here shortly before D-Day.

How we envied the young pilots, as they climbed and rolled these beautiful machines, and we loved the roar of the Rolls Royce Merlin engines as they zoomed over our heads.

Watching from our place of observation late one afternoon, we noticed an RAF lorry driving slowly around the perimeter of the airfield. It stopped and the driver and his companion climbed out, for reasons unknown. We glanced to the rear of our vantage point as the familiar sound of a Spitfire was heard coming into land.

It banked slowly around Lancing College, lowered the undercarriage, then throttled back and lined up for a routine landing. To our horror we realised that it was on a collision course with the lorry and, climbing to our feet, Mike and I waved and shouted for all our worth to try and attract the pilot's attention.

Needless to say our efforts went unseen and, as we watched mesmerised, the Spitfire clipped the top of the lorry tearing off both landing wheels in the process, and with an almighty screech it skidded across the grass landing area, making a deep furrow in the grass as it did so.

We were relieved when the pilot climbed from the cockpit and appeared unhurt, ripping off his flying helmet and throwing it down in obvious frustration and anger. Meanwhile crash tenders and a fire engine raced to the scene, but thankfully were not required.

At night I would often lie awake, listening to the drone of RAF bombers passing overhead, as they took the war to the heart of Germany, bombing their cities in retaliation for the Blitz on ours, some two years previously. During the day further sounds of heavy aircraft engines filled the sky, as huge formations of B17s (Flying Fortresses) continued the bombing, sustaining heavy losses in the process.

We craned our necks to watch the long vapour trails left by hundreds of these American planes, as they flew high overhead towards their target. Their return a few hours later would often be followed by stragglers, flying very low with smoke trailing from one or more engines and, in some cases, it was possible to see large pieces of tail or wing missing, as the pilot struggled to keep the aircraft flying. One B17 actually crash-landed at Shoreham Airport, after being badly shot up during a bombing mission.

Lancing boasted two cinemas at that time, the newly built Luxor and the antiquated Regal in Penhill Road. Mike and I would sally forth after school, clutching our packets of jam sandwiches for tea which we would munch between pictures. If we really enjoyed the main feature, we usually stayed to see it around a second time - that is, provided we were not too late returning home. This was usually no problem in the summer, as with double summertime in force, it remained light until 10 or 11 p.m. We also liked to get our money's worth for our 6d (2½p).

It was possible to actually creep into the Regal without parting with that vast sum. The side exit doors would be opened at the end of the first performance, mainly to let the fog of cigarette smoke disperse. We would wait until the usherette had her back turned, or was flirting with a soldier in the audience, then tiptoe in and slide into the nearest empty seats.

Sometimes we were spotted by a mean spirited character sitting in the stalls and our entrance would be made known to the usherette or manager. Then our exit would be made rather hurriedly and the doors would clang shut behind us.

Our favourite heroes were real action men: John Wayne (starring in *Stagecoach*); Spencer Tracy (*Captain Courageous and Boys Town*); James Cagney (*Angels with Dirty Faces*).

Laughter was provided by - Old Mother Riley, Laurel and Hardy, and our favourite, George Formby.

We always thought he was speaking directly at us, when at the end of each picture, he would look straight at the camera, wink and give his gormless smile whilst tendering his catch phrase, "Turned out nice again, in't it?"

"Tarzan," Johnny Weismuller, never let us down. He even tackled a plane load of German paratroopers single handed! What SS Storm-troopers were doing in darkest Africa, I never could quite fathom. However, they all came to nice gory ends, befitting their kind, being eaten by crocs or sucked down in the swamps, whilst Cheetah the chimp bounced up and down with glee, enjoying their fate as much as we did. We were enthralled with Tarzan's skill in turning a herd of stampeding elephants away with his one simple jungle wail "*Umgoer*".

On the way home from that film, we thought we would try this out on the herd of Friesian cows in a field nearby. *"Umgoer, Umgoer,"* we called over the fence, at these silly animals, who just looked up, turned their heads in our direction and continued chewing.

I didn't like to be beaten by a lot of stupid cows, so the following day I thought I would put my new found skill into practice again. As I passed by the bakers shop I noticed a small pekinese dog tied up by its leash. I stopped, pointed my finger at this animal and demanded in my best Lord of the Jungle tone, *"Umgoer, Umgoer"*.

The little monster drew back its lips, snarled, then leapt straight at me, yapping and straining on its lead to reach me. As I stepped back, the owner - a rather portly middle aged lady - came out of the shop doorway, brandishing her walking stick.

"Leave my Che-Che alone, you cruel little boy," she shouted at me, waving her cane.

I knew what Tarzan would do in circumstances like this, so without further ado, I glared up at this intruder, cupped by hands to the side of my mouth, threw back my head and cried out in jungle fashion, "AH AH AH AH AH."

Then I beat a very hasty retreat!

Chapter Four

The WVS (now WRVS) performed sterling work during the war, as they indeed still do today. They would supervise evacuees, as already mentioned, and provide care and comfort for people whose homes had been bombed.

Two of these stalwart ladies drove an American style pre-war sedan, of unknown vintage or origin, which they used in the course of their duties. The parts for this car were non-existent as the war moved on, and the local garage cursed each time this huge vehicle was brought in for repairs.

We learnt to recognise the sound from this particular engine, as it wheezed and coughed along the almost deserted roads, and Michael and I would wave to the two middle-aged lady occupants, as they drove by.

One afternoon on the way home from school, the unmistakable sound of this ancient motor caught our ears. We stopped walking and turned around, expecting to see this all too familiar vehicle appear around the corner. The rattling and wheezing intensified and then, to our amazement, a solitary wheel rolled into view, followed by the incredible sight of the car balancing on three wheels, its front offside one now rolling along the footpath.

Mike and I just shook with laughter as the two dear ladies smiling and waving at us, passed by oblivious to the fact that their car had become a three-wheeler. Thankfully, they always drove very slowly and, as they reached the next bend in the road, gravity came to the fore. With a resounding crash the front of the car tipped onto the hub, tearing a long gash in the tarmac, as it came to a grinding halt. We ran to the scene of the strange accident as the two ladies climbed out unhurt looking none the worse for their ordeal.

"Have you two boys seen a car wheel?" enquired one of these matronly ladies.

We clasped our hands over our mouths to hide our giggles and, suppressing our laughter, pointed to the missing tyre some 200 yards away.

Hit and run raiders frequently harassed coastal towns. They would fly low across the channel, keeping just above the wave tops to avoid detection by radar, then drop their bombs, or machine gun anything in sight, before warnings could be sounded, by which time they had all but disappeared.

One afternoon, after Dad had completed his business in Worthing, we were driving along the coast road towards Lancing. The wide expanse of wasteland (now Brooklands) was a vast array of metal poles resembling scaffolding, erected as a deterrent for enemy gliders. Between this jungle of steel could be seen fishing boats and dinghies, once housed on the beach, but now sadly rotting with neglect. A large pile of flat-bottomed motor and paddle boats from the pre-war Beach House boating lake, also lay like discarded toys hastily thrown away as if by some unruly child.

Nearing the junction with Western Road in Lancing I noticed a soldier in uniform, waving furiously at us. Dad raised his hand from the steering wheel, as if in recognition, and waved back. As we passed this khaki clad figure, I turned to look closer and, pressing my nose hard against the glass, was puzzled to see him mouthing words in our direction, whilst still signalling frantically with his arms. My final glimpse of this strange figure was to see him lying face down upon the hard unwelcome pavement. Before I could make my observations known to my father, a further strange sight met my inquisitive gaze.

Sparks and chips of pavement were flying in all directions, alongside the van, but before I could open my mouth to question these strange sights, an enormous roar seemed to fill the inside of the van, as a Messerschmit 109 fighter roared overhead, with all guns blazing, then thankfully climbed away out of our line of vision.

I turned towards dad, now clutching the steering wheel tightly with both hands, his ashen face staring fixedly ahead.

"Dad, I think that soldier was trying to tell us something," I said with a trembling voice.

In the early spring of 1944, allied military activity on the south coast increased by the day, and the recreation ground became a huge camp for Canadian soldiers again in preparation for D-Day. We made friends with a lot of these troops and they tried to teach us to play baseball, which we thought very sissy, and likened it to a girl's game of rounders.

One of the Canadians, Doug Clarke from Saskatchewan, became a close friend of the family, and would keep me enthralled with tales of his lumberjack days in the backwoods of Canada. We were all sorry when his unit was transferred to Bexhill prior to the D-Day landings. He kept in touch, however, and always signed his letters "from your adopted son Doug".

Many months went by with not a word, and we feared the worst, knowing that the Canadians had sustained heavy losses. However shortly after VE-Day Doug appeared on our doorstep, with a very pretty girl holding his arm, whom he introduced as his bride to be.

Childlike, I questioned him about his exploits in France. "Did you kill any Germans?" I asked without thinking about the implications.

He looked very hesitant then, after a pause, said rather quietly, "Perhaps I did! There were so many of them!"

Brighton Road, Worthing looking east towards Lancing, 1940
(Now Brooklands)

Brooklands looking north

Worthing Pier, 1940

Oh, to be allowed through that wire

Anti aircraft guns, Worthing seafront
(Note missing bulb from lamp post)

Beach House Promenade
(Note "Pill Box" at Splash Point)

Old Town Hall, and pill box Worthing 1940s

Marine Parade, Worthing, 1940s

I was unable to extract any further information from him, and even at my age, sensed that he wanted to put these traumatic experiences behind him.

Dad was allowed a very meagre ration of precious petrol for delivering in the van and, as he reported to Head Office once a week, I would often go along for the ride into Worthing. Apart from military vehicles and the occasional bus or trade vehicle, the roads remained deserted of traffic, and as we drove along the seafront I would catch a glimpse of aircraft wreckage and such like, littering the high water mark of the beach, tantalising beyond reach, owing to large concrete blocks and barbed wire entwined between, which stretched the entire length of the foreshore.

Oh, to be allowed through that wire! What a feast of souvenirs awaited us, but the authorities kept curious children at bay, with warning notices that all beaches were mined.

A large section of the pier was blown up by the army when invasion was a strong possibility, and the wreckage appeared like Neptune's trident arising from the waves which crashed against it, as the remainder stood in isolation awaiting happier times.

With so much of the town occupied by the military, road blocks were set up and identity cards had to be shown before we were allowed to continue. Tanks and armoured vehicles filled many roads, and Marine Parade in Worthing appeared to be covered with army ambulances, parked like sardines, with distinct red crosses emblazoned on their roofs and doors.

We were not aware at the time, but Warnes Hotel had been converted as headquarters of the RAMC (Royal Army Medical Corps) in readiness for the large number of casualties expected.

In the small hours of June 6 1944 my family was awakened by the roar of hundreds of aircraft engines passing overhead.

"Something big is on!" exclaimed my father.

The following morning we learned from the BBC that this really was the big one, with Allied troops storming ashore on the

Normandy beaches, including our Canadians who had left some days previously.

Our school grapevine was also humming with the news that an aircraft had crashed at Sompting during the night. Jumping on our bikes immediately after school, we hurriedly cycled along to the scene of the crash, hoping for more souvenirs.

There in a field, slightly to the west of Sompting Church, was a "Horsa" glider, with black and white stripes painted on its wings and fuselage to indicate that was an Allied aircraft.

The glider, which was virtually intact, had crash-landed after breaking its tow rope during the night. Of the crew and airborne troops there was no sign, and the Home Guard and police, unfortunately, kept us from bringing back any mementos.

I often wondered how the pilot managed to land without hitting the church or the elm trees which surrounded the field and if those troops reached Normandy on D-Day minus one.

The news following the Allied invasion of France, was most encouraging and promised, at last, an end to the carnage.

A vast POW (Prisoner of War) camp was constructed in West Street, Sompting, and we would cycle there to gaze over the wall at our captured enemies. To our surprise they didn't look much different from the Canadian troops who had previously occupied the canvas tents they were now living in.

The large yellow diamond or circle stitched to their uniforms was the only indication that they were POW's.

Then, just when we thought it safe to sleep in our beds again, a new ominous sound was heard in the sky - Doodlebugs!

Doodlebugs, V1 flying bombs, Hitler's secret victory weapons, were unleashed in the summer of 1944. The unmistakable sound from these pilotless bombs, was soon familiar to our ears, and we would listen out for the familiar pop popping sound of their rocket motors, as they flew across the sky.

All the while the engine was running there was nothing to fear, but when it started spluttering and eventually stopped, then we took cover wherever possible. The missile would then fall to earth at random, and a huge explosion would follow.

Spitfire and Mustang fighters soared to meet this new threat, and we children waved frantically as they flew low over the roof tops, when returning to their bases at Tangmere and Ford. Occasionally we were rewarded as they waggled their wings in recognition.

In August of that same year, my parents decided to have their first holiday since the war began, and spend this with my father's parents at their home at Emsworth on the Hampshire and Sussex border.

As we alighted from the packed train, which had brought us from Worthing, with sailors and soldiers standing shoulder to shoulder in the corridors, the words of a poster adjoining the ticket office, kept haunting me: "IS YOUR JOURNEY REALLY NECESSARY?"

With some concern I considered these words carefully, and came to the conclusion that, yes, our journey was absolutely necessary, otherwise how else could we possibly reach our destination?

Chapter Five

To describe my grandparents' home, is to journey back to the dawn of the twentieth Century, a home little changed since my father's father brought his young bride to this tiny cottage which would be their home for the duration of their married life. Here, they raised six healthy children, three boys and three girls - my father being the eldest - in conditions which lacked the most simple domestic and sanitary facilities.

Electricity, their sole modern luxury, was only installed in the late 1930s. Their other facilities, or should I say lack of them, remained exactly the same as when the cottage had been built, in about 1840.

Cooking was done on an enormous black cast iron open kitchen range, which also heated the scullery or living room, with a fire constantly blazing summer and winter.

Sanitation was, to say the least, primitive. The loo, or privy as it was known, was a small brick and slate building adjoining the woodshed some ten or twelve feet from the house. It consisted of a plank of wood with a hole cut in the centre, suspended over a large cast iron bucket, into which one would perform the necessary bodily functions. It usually reeked of extra strong disinfectant, which disguised other unpleasant odours, and also served to deter the flies, which were usually in attendance during the warm summer months.

Washing facilities were situated in the far corner of the woodshed. They consisted of one solitary brass tap above a stoneware sink, well stocked with Lifebuoy soap. The water from this tap was always icy cold, even on the hottest summer's day.

The woodshed served not only as a bathroom, but, as the name implies, it also contained logs and kindling wood for the range. As well as this, it was well-stocked with produce from the garden, with racks of apples, pears and vegetables awaiting culinary preparation.

In the opposite corner was a brick and cast iron copper with a wooden lid. This doubled as a family laundry, and also for preserving soft fruits and pickles, which would be boiled prior to bottling.

The garden from whence came all this produce, was more than a garden. Smallholding would be a more apt description. Vegetables of every description were grown in rich profusion. Apple, pear, cherry, plum and even fig trees, spread their foliage, whilst raspberries and strawberries would fill a trug to overflowing.

As if all this vegetation was not enough for my industrious grandparents, livestock - consisting of pigs, chickens and rabbits - was kept to supplement their food rationing, of which they were hardly aware.

During these austere days this oasis of tranquillity appeared as a paradise to me at eight years of age. The final icing on the cake was the small stream running at the end of the garden on which swans and mallards drifted serenely by. As I gazed in awe from between the rushes growing on the riverbank, they would hiss or quack at the small human figure who dared to disturb their quiet seclusion.

On the day that we arrived at my grandparents' home, I ran excitedly in front of my parents, down the narrow path bordered by hawthorns, which led to the cottage. Peering through a gap in the hedge, I espied the familiar figure of my grandfather engaged in preparing food for the animals.

"Hello young shaver," he called out smiling, recognising me as I ran quickly towards him.

"Can I help you with the pigs, and see the rabbits grandad?" I blurted out breathlessly.

"All in good time young man. I haven't said hello to your mum and dad yet," he exclaimed, waving to my parents and sister, who by now had reached the garden.

I climbed the deep well-worn steps and pushed open the door of the cottage which had been left ajar. The heavy lion's head knocker rattled slightly, causing my grandmother to turn away from the kitchen range, and wiping her hands on her pinafore, she smiled with recognition at my entrance.

After the inevitable hugs and kisses had been exchanged between the families, the adults conversation turned to the progress of the war and my uncle's recent activities working at the Portsmouth dockyard, during the preparations for D-Day.

When it was time for lunch, we drew up the old Victorian dining chairs and sat around a solid pine table covered with a damask table cloth, and eagerly awaited the meal which had been prepared for us.

Lifting the heavy iron catch of the oven, cloth in hand, gran revealed a large tin dish containing crisp amber roast potatoes surrounding a leg of succulent pork, the glistening crackling emitting a most appetising aroma. Peas, carrots and cauliflower awaited their turn to be served from soot-encrusted iron pots, simmering on the range.

When my plate was set before me, I swung my legs excitedly beneath the table, but stopped abruptly as an ominous growl came from beneath my feet.

"It's alright, Jock! He won't kick you," grandad reassured the dog, which I had forgotten was there. "He's not used to little boys sitting at the table. You sit still and behave and Jock won't make a sound," he said, giving my mother a knowing wink. Needless to say, my table manners were exemplary after this warning, and I sat hardly daring to move for the remainder of the meal.

When we had finished our lunch, which included a delicious bread and butter pudding for afters, my father and I, together with grandad, went to look at the garden. As we passed by the Anderson shelter, covered in nasturtiums and cornflowers, my father's proffered eye as a warden noticed that it had hardly been used as a refuge from the bombing.

As he jokingly chastised my grandfather for using this shelter as little more than another garden shed, grandad explained with a chuckle: "We haven't had a raid for months now! They appear to have left Pompey and Thorney alone."

That very night I was woken soon after going to bed by my mother shaking me. Sitting up and rubbing the sleep from my eyes, I heard the all too familiar sound of the air raid siren. As we hurriedly made our way to the front door, I remembered my grandfather's words to dad that afternoon, and chuckled to myself as the siren finished its mournful wail.

The garden looked so peaceful in the darkness, lit only by the stars glinting in the warm summer air. One star, however, appeared much brighter than the others and was also moving quickly across the sky. The familiar stuttering sound caught our ears, and by the time we had reached the shelter, red flames could be seen emitting from this flying bomb, which appeared to be heading in our direction.

"It's alright!" explained my father to my rather frightened grandparents, as he shone his torch into the shelter, revealing flower pots, seed trays and the like. "The motor's running, nothing to worry about!"

One at a time we descended into the shelter, crunching pots underfoot. Then my father suddenly called out. "Oh my God, the bloody engine's cutting out!" Giving my mother a push from behind, she fell rather than climbed into the damp semi-buried hide, with dad sliding in behind her, closing the frail wooden door as he did so. "Everybody put their heads down and hands over their necks," he shouted, remembering his ARP training.

1, 2, 3, 4, 5, 6 .... dad started counting the seconds away, as we waited for the inevitable explosion. I raised my head slightly, giggling at the peculiar sight which confronted my eyes in the dull glow of the torchlight: The entire family pressed tightly together and all bent over as if in a rugby scrum or prayer, which by the mutterings issuing forth from beneath our lowered heads, probably were.

....15, 16, 17, 18.... Still counting, my father was by this time also raising his head, awaiting the impact which must surely follow. Then he stopped counting, waited for a minute, then cautiously opened the door. Raising his head very slowly through the entrance, his gaze revealed an empty sky. There followed an expletive which assailed our ears in the shelter. "Where the devil's the bugger gone?"

The following day we learnt from the local police where the so and so really had gone. Two police officers on duty in the square had seen the rocket motor cut out and, as it started its descent, by some miracle had veered away over the roofs of the town and dived, without exploding, into the mud of the harbour. "The bomb disposal boys are digging it out now," they explained.

The harbour fascinated me, with South Street leading right down to the water's edge when the tide was high. The old derelict mill and pond had long fallen into disuse, similarly the oyster beds, for which Emsworth had once been famous.

The fishing smack, *Non Parriel,* was still berthed alongside the wooden jetty, known locally as the Ark, her last cargo of oysters long since unloaded, and her only crew now seagulls and cormorants vying with each other for a place on the rotting taffrail.

Beneath the sea wall were moored the remaining small fishing boats, wooden oars and lugsail their sole means of propulsion, gently rocking with the rising tide. Their owners, elderly fishermen, liked nothing better than to reminisce about pre-war days, when they sailed as crew for Sir Thomas Sopwith, the aviation millionaire, in his J Class yacht *Endeavour*, as he attempted to win the Americas Cup, an elusive prize which always remained beyond his reach.

Their Guernseys still carried the legend *"Endeavour* RYS" (Royal Yacht Squadron) embroidered on many of them.

One delicacy still caught by these old-timers was cockles, and a plateful of these covered liberally with vinegar, was a gourmet

The Quay, Emsworth

The oasis of tranquillity

Lumley Cottages

Grandad and author aged nine

feast indeed.

As if to remind us that war was still being fought, the roar of Mosquito fighter bombers filled the air as they practised take-off and landing on nearby Thorney Island. Only a few months previously, two aircraft had collided in mid-air and crashed into the harbour. Two local lads had made a brave attempt to rescue the crew of one of them, but had unfortunately been driven back by the flames.

I was always sad when it was time to return home to Lancing, the holiday having gone all too quickly. Another winter of war to be tackled, and further months of sharing sleeping arrangements with my sister and mother in the Morrison shelter erected in our living room.

This all steel shelter, bolted together like a large metal table with heavy gauge wire mesh panels on all four sides, provided adequate protection should the house collapse around us, the result of V1 or V2 rocket attacks, the latter which gave no warning of its presence whatsoever.

An unexpected surprise awaited us upon arriving home from Emsworth. A large food parcel sent by my uncle in Canada.

It was just like Christmas, as we excitedly opened the contents. Inside we found tinned cake and fruits, sweets, chewing gum by the box and best of all plain unmarked tins containing delicious red salmon, which my uncle had canned for us.

Just a few days later yet another parcel arrived, this time containing a whole smoked ham, which dad cut in half and asked our local butcher to keep in his cold store, until Christmas.

How lucky we were compared to so many families during those austere years, which seemed to drag on forever.

1945 was the sixth year of war. The radio and newspapers were full of the exciting news as city after city was liberated in France, Belgium and Holland.

By this time I had started scanning the newspapers after dad had finished reading them. Giles cartoons in the *Express* always made me laugh, but on a more sombre note, photos and reports from Belsen and Aushwitz were very disturbing, and I began to realise that war wasn't a game after all.

8th May 1945 VE Day, what a day to remember. The Germans finally surrendered and the war in Europe was over.

We children helped to build an enormous bonfire in the recreation ground and tables and chairs were brought out from neighbouring houses, as the mothers hastily prepare a street party for us. My dad provided free lemonade and ginger beer from large stone jars and uncorked a bottle of Hock, which he had saved from before the war to drink old Hitler's health in hell.

As darkness fell blackout blinds were removed from the windows of the surrounding houses and for the first time that we could remember, artificial light illuminated the street.

The bonfire was set ablaze and we all joined in the merriment, as parents and children danced and sang around the fire. Suddenly I started to feel cold, and shivered with fear and apprehension, expecting at any moment to hear the wail of the siren and a roar of bombers attracted to all this light. But it was not be heard again. It finally was the last all clear.

Chapter Six

With the long summer holiday from school approaching in that final year of war, I persuaded my parents to let me return to Emsworth and spend the best part of August at this paradise which I had discovered - subject of course to my grandparents tolerating a nine-year-old for several weeks.

I was overjoyed when they wrote and said that I could stay for as long as I wanted. With some misgivings, my father put me on the train at Worthing and, feeling very grown up, I counted the stations as they went by until eventually the train stopped at Emsworth.

Alighting from the carriage with my small case clasped in my hand, I walked towards my destination about a mile away, a route I knew by heart. As excitement mounted within me at this great adventure I was embarking upon alone, I ran down the lane towards the familiar cottage. A warm welcome awaiting me.

The following morning I awoke early, and crawling across the top of the bed, I pushed aside the curtains and knelt at the small gabled window. Shielding my eyes from the bright sunlight, the vista of the garden below appeared as a kaleidoscope of colour. The Beauty of Bath apples were already ripening on the branches beneath the window, whilst plums and pears weighed down the boughs of nearby trees.

At the far end of the garden the familiar figure of my grandfather could be seen mixing buckets of food for the noisy pigs, squealing and grunting in anticipation of their morning meal.

Hurriedly climbing out of bed and banging my knee on the marble top wash stand as I did so, I poured some water from the large jug into the matching china bowl, and quickly washed my face and hands.

After pulling on my grey flannel shirt and shorts, I made my way down the stairs which led to the scullery, clutching the knotted rope which served as a bannister tightly in my small hand - it knocked against the wood panelling with every step.

Reaching the bottom, I lifted the latch and opened the scullery door. A delightful aroma of wood smoke and bacon greeted my nostrils. Gran was busy as usual tending the fire, and held a large frying pan sizzling with rashers of bacon.

"You're up early, dear!" she said smiling. "Would you like to go and get an egg for your breakfast?"

I knew exactly what she meant and, needing no further bidding, I put on my shoes and hurried out into the garden towards the hen house adjoining the wall of the cottage. The Light Sussex and Rhode Island Red hens clucked impatiently at me, thinking I had brought their meal, whilst I was seeking mine. I worked my way around to the side of the coop, and it was a simple matter to lift the wooden flap of the nesting box and remove a warm egg or two from the nest of straw within.

As I sat eating my breakfast, relishing every mouthful, with egg yolk dribbling down my chin, I had time to observe my surroundings in this sparsely furnished room. Above the kitchen range, gleaming with black leading, was a thick timber mantel. Pride of place in the centre sat a large tin clock adorned with sheikhs and camels painted red, black and gold, it bore the legend on the reverse "Victory V Lozenges"! On either side of the time-piece were two brass shell cases which grandad had brought back from France in 1918.

Grandad's chair was nearest the fire and was covered with numerous cushions in a variety of materials. Beneath the seat a pair of well-worn felt slippers poked out, awaiting their owner's return.

The walls always intrigued me, being covered in layers of old newspapers, prior to having been painted with cream distemper.

If you looked closely, it was possible to discern type and photos showing through numerous coats of paint applied over many years.

Briar pipes were allotted their regimental places in a rack fixed to the wall at the side of the grate, and completing this male domain was a hearthrug made from offcuts of cloth in a multitude of colours.

With breakfast over, it was time to join my grandfather and help with the animals, who were clamouring to be fed their morning meal. As I made my way into the garden I paused to admire the delightful view across the neighbouring field to Lumley and the picturesque cottages bordering the waters edge beyond. The tide was full and terns, or sea swallows as we called them, would dive almost vertically to catch whitebait, shimmering like glass crystals on the smooth surface of the water.

Grandad had finished feeding the pigs when I arrived and was busy mixing a mash for the hungry chickens and rabbits. Close by, Jock the dog was ferreting beneath the base of the timber shed which housed bran and meal stored in old jute sacks.

"He can smell those damned rats," he explained, eyeing Jock, who was vigorously scratching a hole with his front paws.

"I'll have to put down some more traps for the blighters, or they'll be into the sacks!" he explained, giving the mash a final stir.

The food supply for these animals came from unwanted or stale produce from the garden. Very little was wasted, as virtually everthing was recycled - and I do mean everything - waste matter both human and animal would be used to provide a continual cycle of food and energy.

If the waste or peelings were running low, twice a week grandfather would push his wooden barrow around the streets of the town, where baskets of kitchen waste would be awaiting him from various households known to the family. This would be piled in a large heap, close to another brick and iron copper built some distance from the house. After shovels of peelings, potatoes, cabbage leaves and such like had filled the copper, water and bran would be added to complete this concoction. Beneath the copper a fire would be lit, and for fuel an inexhaustible supply of old bicycle tyres (courtesy of the cycle shop in the town square) soon had this swill bubbling away merrily.

Needless to say, I enjoyed this bit, and the more thick black smoke that issued forth from the chimney the better, unless of course grandma had put her washing on the line and the prevailing wind blew in that direction - then it was grandfather and I who could expect the proverbial roasting!

When I tired of helping with the animals, my thoughts turned to the stream and the fish and eels therein. How to catch them was uppermost in my mind, but as fish hooks were, like most commodities, unobtainable, there was only one solution: make my own.

Gran supplied me with a number of 1¼" pins which could be bent on the steel vice in the woodshed. The most difficult part was forming a barb, and this I attempted with a small file. After numerous bruised and bloodied fingers, my task was finished - along with my patience!

A ball of garden twine made a superb fishing line, whilst a couple of rusty ³/₈" nuts procured from a box of odds and ends, served as a make-shift weight. There remained just the bait, which was easily obtained by digging in the rich dark soil. In no time my jam jar was half full of thick juicy earthworms, ready to tempt the denizens of the deep.

Casting into the stream from the riverbank took a further toll on my patience, but after several feet of twine had wrapped around reeds and fencing, I at last managed to lob my home-made tackle into the water. Sitting on the bank, line clasped tightly in my hand, it was possible to observe some other inhabitants of the river by remaining quiet and immobile. A disturbance and flurry of mud at the water's edge announced the rapid departure of a moorhen, as it literally flew beneath the surface in search of food, foraging with its beak in the mud as it did so. Like a neon sign in flight, a kingfisher soared above the water, then dived with hardly a splash, returning with a small perch or elver clasped tightly in its bill, to alight in the willow trees which bowed their branches in homage to the water and provider of life.

My reverie was interrupted by the sudden tightening of the line in my hand, and as I quickly got to my feet, I felt a strong wriggling and twisting motion as I hauled in my catch excitedly. The water acted as a magnifier and the eel, for such as it was, appeared enormous to my young eyes. With a startled cry I took a step back, oblivious to the low wire fence behind me.

With my hand still tightly clutching the line, I fell backwards into the gully of mud which served as drainage during winter flooding. The eel followed close behind, landed smack on my face, and then proceeded to slither off over my shirt, which had been clean on that very morning.

As I stood up, my prize, now winding itself around my arm, my grandmother, alerted by my cry, came running from the house thinking I had fallen in.

"Look what I've caught, gran!" I shouted triumphantly, holding the eel aloft. The apparition which confronted my grandmother, caused her to scream in horror for her husband. Blood from the eel covered my face and shirt, whilst mud and blood from cuts on my legs mingled together and ran down to my shoes. The make-shift weights had also caught me sharply on the bridge of my nose, causing this to bleed and add to the general mayhem.

Chapter Seven

Tom the bookies' runner would call at my grandparent's cottage at least once a week, to collect bets from my grandmother to be placed on the gee gees, or racing circuit, which returned to operation during the latter part of the war.

I was intrigued as she studied the form of her chosen mounts and placed 6d (2½p) or 1/- (5p) each way on various horses. When Tom returned with her winnings, to my delight I would be the recipient of 1/- or occasionally the enormous sum of half a crown (12½p) which she would press into the palm of my hand.

Grandfather's income which derived from the produce he sold, was supplemented by part-time gardening, his main employer being a Royal Navy commander, who owned a property on the outskirts of Emsworth.

"Would you like to go with grandad today?"asked my grandmother one morning, as I sat finishing my breakfast.

"Yes please gran!" I answered, stuffing another piece of fried bread into my mouth.

As we made our way through the town, we were greeted by passers-by who recognised the familiar figure of my grandfather pushing his barrow, whilst Jock and I walked alongside towards our destination.

"I see you've got an assistant with you today!" exclaimed one lady, smiling down at me. "You must be very proud of him," she continued. Grandad nodded his head in agreement and smiled.

Leaving the Portsmouth Road behind, we entered a lane running almost parallel with the road, and the wheels of the cart creaked in protest at the uneven surface. After walking for about ten minutes we stopped outside a large detached double-fronted residence, and grandad unlatched the heavy wooden five-barred gate, which led to the driveway. The house appeared rather forbidding, with most of the windows firmly shuttered. Dense foliage grew against the walls and wound itself around pipes and guttering.

"Does anyone live here grandad?" I enquired.

"Not at the moment they don't," he replied. "The Commander's serving in the Far East and the family have gone away for the duration of the war," he continued, as we made our way to the side of the house.

Upon reaching a brick and rendered building, a few yards from the main house, my grandfather extracted a key from his waistcoat pocket and unlocked the door. The door swung open and as my eyes grew accustomed to the dark interior, I noticed a vast array of garden tools and implements hanging and propped up against the wall of the workshop.

"Have we got to use all of these?" I exclaimed in dismay.

"Not all at once, young shaver. We've just the grass to cut today and do a bit of weeding! This is what I need today," he explained, taking a long-handled scythe from its stand against the wall.

He turned towards the nearby bench and selected a hone (or rasp) and, tilting the scythe on end, he commenced honing the edge of the blade.

"While I'm sharpening this, why don't you go and have a peep in that window over there!" he said, pausing and pointing with the hone at another outbuilding about twenty feet away.

"Are there more tools in there grandad?" I enquired.

"You'll see!" he answered smiling.

Puzzled and my curiosity aroused, I hastened across to this mysterious building and attempted to reach the window sill. I glanced around for something to stand on and, as luck would have it, I found an empty wooden crate of the correct proportions leaning against the nearby wall. Placing this in position, I climbed up, cupped one hand over the top of my eyes and gazed at the interior and contents within.

My astonishment caused me to nearly lose my balance, as a veritable Aladdin's cave of toys and models confronted me. There was a huge model yacht, with sails fully set, and two authentic pedal racing cars, with chrome spoke wheels, glass windscreens and even large roundels painted with their racing numbers on their bonnets and doors. Cricket bats and stumps leaned against the wall, whilst in the far corner a beautifully carved and painted rocking horse glared at me with realistic eyes, as I stared in disbelief and admiration. To complete this treasure house, finely detailed model aircraft, hung suspended over a superb railway layout such as I had only ever seen in pre-war magazines.

"Well, what do you think of that?"

My grandfather's voice and sudden approach made me start and I turned away from the window and cried out excitedly, "Oh, grandad, can we go inside? PLEASE!"

"'Fraid not old lad, I don't have a key for the playroom and the Commander's two boys haven't been near for several years," he explained. "Anyhow, this isn't getting the work done is it, and I thought you were going to give me a hand?" he said, chuckling slightly, his hands clasping the handle of the scythe.

Jumping down from the box, I followed him and Jock to the rear of the house, my mind now far away from grass cutting and longing for a chance to examine some of the delights I had just seen.

My thoughts were soon turned in another direction for, as we reached the back of the house, a garden of vast and magnificent proportions met my eyes.

Several acres of land had been landscaped with ornamental trees, shrubs and conifers, in numerous variety. The lawn leading from a balustraded terrace was the size of four tennis courts, whilst beyond this was a large orchard of fruit trees, heavily laden and swaying in the moderate breeze which was blowing from the harbour beyond.

Upon reaching the lawn I realised why grandad had brought the scythe, for the grass was sadly neglected and moved not unlike waves on the seashore, driven by the wind.

"Haven't been up here for a couple of weeks and look how the damned stuff has grown!" exclaimed my grandfather, in an exasperated tone, whilst removing his jacket and commencing to roll up his sleeves.

"It's going to take best part of the day to cut this lot!" he said, spitting on the palms of his hands, before gripping the scythe in readiness. "Would you like to rake the grass into piles as I cut?" he asked. "But keep well back from the blade as I swing, it's now very sharp. The rake is leaning against that magnolia tree over there," he said pointing. "I must have forgotten to put it away the last time I was here. Perhaps I'm getting forgetful in my old age," he chuckled.

Time passed quickly in the warm sunshine, as scent from the newly cut grass pervaded the air. "Time for lunch young shaver," called out my grandfather, removing his old Panama hat and mopping his brow. I dropped my rake and ran across to him at the far end of the lawn. We sat down beneath a row of crab apple trees, their branches hung with tiny fruits resembling clusters of Christmas decorations in a myriad of colours.

Munching our sandwiches which gran had provided, my mind wandered back to the playroom and the treasure house of toys, the like of which I had never seen.

"Grandad," I said, looking up at his weather-beaten face, his grey hair protruding from beneath the old Panama and his thick walrus moustache now showing signs of cheese particles. "Grandad," I repeated, "the Commander must be very rich."

He didn't answer for a few seconds, then, slowly placing his arm around my shoulders replied, smiling slightly, "Not as rich as I am young man." Noting the puzzled expression on my face, he continued by saying, "I have all the wealth a man requires."

This philosophy was lost on me at nine years of age and my bemused expression must have shown on my young face, as he looked fondly at me and went on, "One day, when you're a grandad yourself, you will understand. Now, what about another sandwich?"

"Grandad," I questioned again.

"Now what is it, you young scallywag," he laughed, a slight irritation creeping into his voice.

"Grandad, I wish I could stay with you and granny for always, I don't want to go back to Lancing," I replied wistfully.

"Your mum and dad wouldn't think much of that now, would they?" he answered, clearing his throat with a slight cough. "Besides, they will be here next week to take you home." Seeing my crestfallen face, he turned slightly towards me and, with his eyes looking deep into mine said, gently, "I'll tell your mum and dad that you can come and stay with us any time you like and perhaps next year you can have a look inside that playroom over there."

I was not to know then, but my beloved grandfather would not live to see another summer, for he was to die suddenly in February of the following year, whilst tending his livestock.

"Come on young man, finish your lunch or we shall never get this grass cut in time!" he said, wiping his moustache on his bare arm. "By the way, we mustn't forget to stop at Smith and Vospers on the way home - your gran wants some stale cakes for the trifle on Sunday."

In the small hours of 15th August I was awakened by a strange noise. Climbing from my bed in the darkness, I pushed open the window to be greeted by the most extraordinary sound. From nearby Langstone Harbour and as far away as Portsmouth, could be heard the most incredible choir of ships horns, sirens and whistles, all blowing off steam with shrill whoops and shrieks, which echoed throughout the still summer night in a riotous symphony of noise.

My grandparents, who were also awake, came smiling into my room. "It's all over!" said grandad. "The Japs have finally surrendered! This bloody war is finished at last!" he said solemnly.

For once my grandmother didn't rebuke him for swearing."Get

dressed and we will go up to the square and see what's going on," they said.

Needing no further bidding I hurriedly threw on my clothes and followed them into the garden and the lane leading to the High Street.

As we approached the town the noise from the ships appeared louder, and above this din new sounds were making themselves heard. The town band was out in force, or should I say what passed for a band. Tin baths served as drums, bugles and trumpets were being blown if not played, and even an old piano was mounted on a low hand cart, as local characters formed a procession, increasing in volume by the minute.

Scores of people followed behind, including members of the armed forces of several nationalities. French sailors, red pom poms on their hats, grabbed hold of the girls as they passed, laughing and kissing them as they made their way towards the town centre.

The two pubs in the square had thrown open their doors, licensing hours totally ignored, as even the local bobbies joined in the gaiety. Soldiers and sailors climbed lamp posts and nearby buildings to raise flags of the victorious Allies.

The band had by now sorted out the real musicians, including a rather tipsy pianist, and dancing and singing began in earnest around a huge bonfire blazing in the square.

Gazing in awe at this never to be forgotten scene, it was difficult for me to appreciate that, after six long years, this country really was at peace and the euphoria which I was witnessing, and which was being repeated throughout the land, would herald a return to a way of life totally unknown to a generation of children, reared in wartime.

The singing of the joyous crowds reached a crescendo and, as the words of the song reached my ears, their simple message seemed to convey the true meaning of peace at last for children everywhere.

"Jimmy will go to sleep in his own little room again!"

Chapter Eight

More than half a century has passed since the events I have described took place and yet my story would be incomplete without the following sequel which happened in June 1994 when my wife and I were privileged to witness the commemoration of the D-Day landings by the allied forces, from the deck of the magnificent Cunarder *QE2*.

On 5th June upon reaching Southampton and entering the departure lounge, we felt conspicuous and somewhat embarrassed to be included with all these veterans from the United States, Canada and Great Britain. Why on earth had we come, I pondered, as we jostled amongst these elderly men, many stooped with age, but all of them proudly displaying their campaign medals, which gleamed from meticulous care and polishing and which were protected from the rain which had threatened all day.

The following morning, dawned bright and sunny and, as is our custom, my wife and I rose early and made our way to the boat deck to enjoy the warm sunshine, which sparkled on the green waters of the Solent. Many of the veterans were also early risers and as we passed some of them, exchanging pleasantries and small talk, it was inevitable that I should tender that old wartime maxim to an obvious American veteran: "Got any gum chum?" I asked.

My wife looked away embarrassed, chiding me for my rudeness, but her admonishments went unnoticed as this elderly Yank exclaimed, "Say, I haven't heard that expression in years. "Would you have been one of those Limey kids way back in '44?"

I confessed my guilt, as he shook our hands warmly and introduced us to his middle-aged son, explaining that they came from Chattanooga. "I expect you've heard of it," he said smiling.

"Sounds familiar," I answered. "But pardon me, did you come on the Choo Choo?" We all burst out laughing.

"Do you remember what we called you,* when you were here the last time?" I asked cheekily.

"How could I possibly forget!" he laughed. "But at least I'm over here again," he went on, laughing even more, with a mischievous glint in his eyes, belying his years. Several of his friends joined us, demanding to know what all the laughter was about. He introduced us, explaining how some of them had sailed to this country in 1943 by way of the *Queen Mary*, and their 9th Bomber Group had taken part in the bombing of Normandy fifty years previously. We pointed out that we felt like intruders, on their nostalgic day, and how we had only been small children during the war.

My wife explained that she lived in London in 1940 and had lost her two-year-old sister and an aunt in the Blitz, prior to being evacuated to Devon. She went on to recall how at Christmas 1943 she had walked with her brother several miles to an American camp, for a party that the GIs were giving for the children, and how she had tasted ice cream for the very first time. "You kids had a rough time of it, that's for sure," said one of these grey-haired veterans.

We prepared to walk away and take our leave, but before we could say our farewells, he pulled his hand from his pocket and pressed two small gilt badges into our hands. "You two are as much veterans of the war as we are," he said withdrawing his hand from ours and then added, "Give these to your grandchildren someday."

We looked down at these badges in the palms of our hands, and their legend proclaiming "D-Day Veteran 1944 - 1994". Before we could thank him for our final and ultimate war souvenirs, he had turned away and rejoined his friends as they walked further along the deck, laughing and fooling around in the manner of their youth, when together with their Canadian and British comrades they had struck the first blow to liberate Europe from tyranny.

* *Overpaid, oversexed and over here*

Our final glimpse, their backs now towards us, was of six short words printed on their anoraks: *"All gave some some gave all."*

The following evening we were entertained by a star, not only of stage, radio and TV but a World War II veteran in her own right. Dame Vera Lynn.

As the theatre lights dimmed and she commenced singing those never-to-be-forgotten wartime melodies, the years rolled away and I was that small mischievous little boy again, sitting huddled around the fire with my family, a hot mug of inevitable cocoa clasped in my hand, listening to the forces' sweetheart singing our favourite songs over the airwaves of our wireless.

I glanced around the theatre as the audience joined in the singing, just as they had done all those years ago and yes, even the young set, stewards, waitresses and crew members, were singing heartily. A generation unborn then - and, thank God,- a generation who had never known total war - were caught up in this atmosphere of togetherness and comradeship of which I, like thousands of other wartime children, had been a part of.

As the audience rose as one to give Vera Lynn a much deserved standing ovation, I knew without any doubt why we had come on this trip.

We did meet again, one sunny day.

Epilogue

I consider myself extremely fortunate, that in the midst of my wartime childhood, I was to discover a peace and appreciation of country and wildlife that has remained with me throughout my life and I shall always treasure in my heart the love and kindness afforded me by my late grandparents, together with the simplicity of their delightful home.

Sadly, modern day progress has destroyed so much of the past and inherent beauty. The cottage has been demolished, and where once I climbed pear and apple trees, waving at my grandparents far below, houses and roads now abound. Swans and ducks have long since departed the stream which now trickles beneath the Emsworth by-pass, only the willow trees remain. Lumley cottages have also gone, replaced by modern houses, but the tidal lake still retains its share of sea birds and swans, their harsh cries calling a new generation to witness the beginning of their own *Extraordinary Spring.*

8th June, 1946

To-day, as we celebrate victory, I send this personal message to you and all other boys and girls at school. For you have shared in the hardships and dangers of a total war and you have shared no less in the triumph of the Allied Nations.

I know you will always feel proud to belong to a country which was capable of such supreme effort; proud, too, of parents and elder brothers and sisters who by their courage, endurance and enterprise brought victory. May these qualities be yours as you grow up and join in the common effort to establish among the nations of the world unity and peace.

George R.I.

This certificate was given to all wartime children to coincide with the Victory Parade in London, June 1946